DEBORAH MADISON

Vegetarian
Every Day

Recipes, Tips, and Inspirations

2011

UNIVERSE

Published by UNIVERSE PUBLISHING
A Division of Rizzoli International Publications, Inc.
300 Park Avenue South
New York, NY 10010
www.rizzoliusa.com

Equinox, solstice, and full moon dates are
given according to Eastern Standard Time
or Eastern Daylight Saving Time as applicable.

Design by Stislow Design
Printed in Hong Kong, PRC

A HOME-COOKED MEAL IS MORE THAN JUST FOOD. There is a fundamental joy in cooking, born of the pleasure of using our senses—rustling our fingers through a bunch of herbs, listening to the sizzle of onions, inhaling the fragrance of olive oil the moment it hits hot pasta. *Vegetarian Every Day 2011*, like all my books, is not intended only for vegetarians. It's for everyone interested in learning how to cook vegetables creatively, healthfully, and passionately.

Today there's much more awareness about all aspects of the foods on our tables and their effects on our health. More than ever it matters that people take their vegetables seriously. Despite the fact that a sweet potato is loaded with beta-carotene, my recipes are for those of us who like to eat, who care about what we eat, and who view cooking and eating together as one of life's pleasures.

Vegetables are at the heart of my cooking and today there's a fetching plethora available in farmers' markets and on our market shelves. Most of the time I happily make a meal from what others place on the side of the plate without even thinking of it as vegetarian. Rather than looking for meat substitutes, these recipes follow the calendar, making use of each season's fresh vegetables and herbs. Some are simple, others more complex, but all are written with an eye toward the seasonality of produce.

Whether you are a committed vegetarian or simply looking for a way to incorporate more meatless meals into your cooking, I hope you will find in *Vegetarian Every Day 2011* a healthful year of delicious eating.

~Deborah Madison

DECEMBER 2010 / JANUARY 2011

Monday   27

Tuesday   28

Wednesday   29

Thursday   30

Friday   31

Saturday   1

New Year's Day

Sunday   2

DECEMBER 2010

S	M	T	W	T	F	S
			1	2	3	4
5	6	7	8	9	10	11
12	13	14	15	16	17	18
19	20	21	22	23	24	25
26	27	28	29	30	31	

JANUARY 2011

S	M	T	W	T	F	S
						1
2	3	4	5	6	7	8
9	10	11	12	13	14	15
16	17	18	19	20	21	22
23	24	25	26	27	28	29
30	31					

Winter Portobello Mushroom Stew

A QUICK AND RELIABLE STEW with big flavors and many applications, this is best made with Mushroom Stock (see below), but not impossible without it. Serve with soft polenta, mashed potatoes, pasta, or over toast.

Serves 4

$1/4$ CUP OLIVE OIL

1 LARGE ONION, DICED

2 TSPS CHOPPED ROSEMARY

SALT AND FRESHLY GROUND
   BLACK PEPPER

2 PINCHES RED PEPPER FLAKES

$1/2$ LB PORTOBELLO
   MUSHROOMS, GILLS
   REMOVED, SLICED $3/8$ INCH
   THICK

1 LB LARGE WHITE
   MUSHROOMS, THICKLY
   SLICED

2 GARLIC CLOVES, MINCED

3 TBSPS TOMATO PASTE

$1 1/2$ CUPS MUSHROOM
   STOCK (SEE RIGHT) OR
   WATER

1 TSP SHERRY VINEGAR

1 TBSP BUTTER

2 TBSPS CHOPPED PARSLEY
   OR TARRAGON

Heat 1 tablespoon of the oil in a large skillet over medium heat. Add the onion and rosemary and cook, stirring occasionally, until lightly browned, about 12 minutes. Season with salt, pepper, and red pepper flakes and remove to a bowl.

Return the pan to medium heat and add half the remaining oil. When hot, add the portobello mushrooms and sauté until browned, about 5 minutes. Add them to the onions and repeat with remaining oil and white mushrooms. Return everything to the pan and add the garlic, tomato paste, stock, and vinegar. Simmer gently for 12 to 15 minutes, then swirl in the butter. Add the parsley, taste for salt, and season with pepper.

Mushroom Stock: Cover $1/4$ cup dried porcini mushrooms with $1 1/2$ cups boiling water; set aside. Heat 2 teaspoons of olive oil in a saucepan with 1 coarsely chopped onion, 1 chopped carrot, 1 clove of garlic, and 2 sliced mushrooms (as well as any trimmings). Sauté over high heat until well browned, about 10 minutes. Reduce the heat to medium and work in 2 teaspoons tomato paste, 1 teaspoon dried marjoram, and 1 tablespoon flour. Stir in $1/2$ cup dry red or white wine and simmer until the wine is reduced, about 3 minutes. Add the porcini and their soaking water, $1/2$ teaspoon salt, freshly ground pepper, 1 teaspoon red wine vinegar and simmer for 20 minutes. Strain and remove dried mushrooms before use. Makes about 1 cup.

JANUARY

Monday 3

Tuesday 4

Wednesday 5

Thursday 6

Friday 7

Saturday 8

Sunday 9

JANUARY

S	M	T	W	T	F	S
						1
2	3	4	5	6	7	8
9	10	11	12	13	14	15
16	17	18	19	20	21	22
23	24	25	26	27	28	29
30	31					

FEBRUARY

S	M	T	W	T	F	S
		1	2	3	4	5
6	7	8	9	10	11	12
13	14	15	16	17	18	19
20	21	22	23	24	25	26
27	28					

JANUARY

Monday   **10**

Tuesday   **11**

Wednesday   **12**

Thursday   **13**

Friday   **14**

Saturday   **15**

Sunday   **16**

JANUARY

S	M	T	W	T	F	S
						1
2	3	4	5	6	7	8
9	10	11	12	13	14	15
16	17	18	19	20	21	22
23	24	25	26	27	28	29
30	31					

FEBRUARY

S	M	T	W	T	F	S
		1	2	3	4	5
6	7	8	9	10	11	12
13	14	15	16	17	18	19
20	21	22	23	24	25	26
27	28					

Composed Salad of Winter Vegetables with Romesco Sauce

ROMESCO, a Catalan sauce combining the essences of grilled peppers, tomatoes, and roasted nuts, is utterly vivid. It's as good atop this salad of winter vegetables as it is with warm chickpeas, large white beans, or on virtually any grilled vegetable.

Serves 4 to 6

ROMESCO SAUCE (SEE RIGHT)

1 SMALL CAULIFLOWER, BROKEN INTO FLORETS AND STEAMED

2 CARROTS, SLICED ON THE DIAGONAL AND STEAMED

3 RED POTATOES, BOILED AND SLICED

4 SMALL RED OR GOLDEN BEETS, ROASTED, PEELED, AND QUARTERED

3 HARD-COOKED EGGS, QUARTERED

12 SICILIAN GREEN OLIVES

CHOPPED PARSLEY

Make the sauce and thin it with enough water to give it the texture of thick cream. Arrange the cooked vegetables attractively with the eggs and olives, then spoon the sauce over or around the plate, and top with parsley.

Romesco Sauce: Fry 1 slice country-style white bread torn into cubes in olive oil until crisp and golden. Grind cooled bread, $^1/_4$ cup toasted almonds, $^1/_4$ cup toasted and peeled hazelnuts, 3 garlic cloves, and 1 to 2 teaspoons red pepper flakes in a food processor. Add 1 tablespoon parsley leaves, salt, freshly cracked pepper, 1 teaspoon paprika, and 1 roasted red pepper. Puree until smooth. With machine running, add $^1/_4$ cup sherry vinegar, then $^1/_2$ cup plus 2 tablespoons extra-virgin olive oil, preferably Spanish. Taste for piquancy and seasoning. Makes about 1 cup.

Potato and Leek Gratin

FEW FOODS ELICIT the rapturous sighs that a golden gratin of potatoes does. Simmering the potatoes and leeks in milk first ensures that your potatoes end up fully tender. Serve with a salad and chilled applesauce.

Serves 4 to 6

1 GARLIC CLOVE AND BUTTER FOR THE DISH

3 LBS RUSSET OR YUKON GOLD POTATOES, PEELED AND VERY THINLY SLICED

1 QUART MILK

1 BAY LEAF

3 THYME SPRIGS OR 2 PINCHES DRIED

3 GARLIC CLOVES, THINLY SLICED

2 LARGE LEEKS, WHITE PARTS ONLY, THINLY SLICED

SALT AND FRESHLY GROUND BLACK PEPPER

GRATED NUTMEG

1 TO 2 CUPS GRATED GRUYÈRE CHEESE

2 TBSPS BUTTER, CUT INTO SMALL PIECES

Preheat the oven to 375. Rub a 9-x-12-inch gratin dish thoroughly with the garlic, then butter, to coat well.

Put the potatoes in a pot with the milk, herbs, sliced garlic, leeks, and 2 teaspoons salt. Slowly bring to a boil, then simmer until the potatoes are barely tender and drain. Discard the herbs.

Make a single layer of potatoes, leeks, and garlic in the dish. Season with pepper and a pinch of nutmeg and cover lightly with cheese. Repeat until all the potatoes and cheese are used up, ending with a layer of cheese. Add enough of the milk to come up to the last layer of potatoes. Dot with butter, then bake until a golden crust has formed on the top, about an hour.

To vary this or other gratins, try using Italian Fontina cheese, Cheddar, Cantal, or in half the amount, Gorgonzola dolcelatte in place of the Gruyère.

Monday 17

Martin Luther King Jr. Day (US)

Tuesday 18

Wednesday 19

Full Moon

Thursday 20

Friday 21

Saturday 22

Sunday 23

JANUARY

S	M	T	W	T	F	S
						1
2	3	4	5	6	7	8
9	10	11	12	13	14	15
16	17	18	19	20	21	22
23	24	25	26	27	28	29
30	31					

FEBRUARY

S	M	T	W	T	F	S
		1	2	3	4	5
6	7	8	9	10	11	12
13	14	15	16	17	18	19
20	21	22	23	24	25	26
27	28					

JANUARY

Monday   24

Tuesday   25

Wednesday   26

Thursday   27

Friday   28

Saturday   29

Sunday   30

JANUARY

S	M	T	W	T	F	S
						1
2	3	4	5	6	7	8
9	10	11	12	13	14	15
16	17	18	19	20	21	22
23	24	25	26	27	28	29
30	31					

FEBRUARY

S	M	T	W	T	F	S
		1	2	3	4	5
6	7	8	9	10	11	12
13	14	15	16	17	18	19
20	21	22	23	24	25	26
27	28					

Mixed Citrus Salad with Avocado

AVOCADOS AND CITRUS FRUIT grow near each other, their seasons overlap, and their textures and tastes are complementary, so it's hardly surprising that they show up together in salads.

Serves 4

1 LIME

2 TANGERINES

2 NAVEL OR BLOOD ORANGES

2 RUBY GRAPEFRUITS

2 RIPE BUT FIRM HASS
    AVOCADOS

1 SHALLOT, FINELY DICED, OR
    2 SCALLIONS, THINLY
    SLICED

1 TBSP FRESH LEMON JUICE

SALT AND FRESHLY GROUND
    WHITE PEPPER

1 TBSP OLIVE OIL

1 TBSP CHOPPED MINT

1 BUNCH WATERCRESS, LARGE
    STEMS REMOVED, OR THE
    INNER LEAVES OF 1 HEAD
    BOSTON LETTUCE

Grate the lime and one of the tangerines and put the zest in a bowl. Peel and section the fruit letting the pieces fall into the bowl. Reserve 1 tablespoon of the juice (and drink the rest).

Slice the avocados into the citrus sections. Combine the shallot with the citrus zest, reserved juice, lemon juice, and $^1/_8$ teaspoon salt; whisk in the oil. Pour the dressing over the fruit, add the mint and a little pepper, and toss gently. Garnish with the watercress or tuck among the lettuce leaves.

Of the various avocados available, the Hass is most commonly seen. Dark green to black with pebbly, rough skin, its flesh is buttery and dense.

JANUARY / FEBRUARY

Monday   **31**

Tuesday   **1**

Wednesday   **2**

Groundhog Day

Thursday   **3**

Chinese New Year

Friday   **4**

Saturday   **5**   Sunday   **6**

JANUARY

S	M	T	W	T	F	S
						1
2	3	4	5	6	7	8
9	10	11	12	13	14	15
16	17	18	19	20	21	22
23	24	25	26	27	28	29
30	31					

FEBRUARY

S	M	T	W	T	F	S
		1	2	3	4	5
6	7	8	9	10	11	12
13	14	15	16	17	18	19
20	21	22	23	24	25	26
27	28					

FEBRUARY

Monday 7

Tuesday 8

Wednesday 9

Thursday 10

Friday 11

Saturday 12

Sunday 13

FEBRUARY

S	M	T	W	T	F	S
		1	2	3	4	5
6	7	8	9	10	11	12
13	14	15	16	17	18	19
20	21	22	23	24	25	26
27	28					

MARCH

S	M	T	W	T	F	S
		1	2	3	4	5
6	7	8	9	10	11	12
13	14	15	16	17	18	19
20	21	22	23	24	25	26
27	28	29	30	31		

Kale with Cannellini Beans

ADDING WHITE BEANS TO GREENS makes a hearty, unpretentious, and fast supper. Serve with garlicky toasts or covered with bread crumbs toasted in olive oil.

Serves 2 to 4

1 ¹/₂ TO 2 LBS KALE OR MIXED GREENS, STEMS AND RIBS REMOVED

SALT AND FRESHLY GROUND BLACK PEPPER

1 SMALL ONION, FINELY DICED

1 ¹/₂ TBSPS OLIVE OIL

2 PLUMP GARLIC CLOVES, MINCED

PINCH RED PEPPER FLAKES

2 TSPS CHOPPED ROSEMARY

¹/₂ CUP DRY WHITE WINE

1 ¹/₃ CUPS COOKED CANNELLINI BEANS, RINSED IF CANNED

FRESHLY GRATED PARMESAN

Simmer the kale in a large pot of boiling, salted water until tender, 7 to 10 minutes. Drain, reserving the cooking water, and chop the leaves. Sauté the onion in the oil with garlic, pepper flakes, and rosemary in a large skillet, for about 3 minutes. Add the wine and cook until reduced to a syrup. Add the beans, kale, and enough of the reserved cooking water to keep the mixture loose. Heat through, taste for salt, season with pepper, and serve with a dusting of Parmesan.

A splash of vinegar or squeeze of lemon is often the secret element that brings a dish to life. This is especially true with foods that are naturally strong in flavor, like the more aggressive greens. That squeeze of lemon or light dousing of vinegar magically sweetens, softens, and sharpens, making everything taste better. Pepper sauce, that ubiquitous seasoning of the South, is one way of getting vinegar on those greens.

Glazed Carrots with Mustard and Honey

MOST CARROTS with greens still attached simply need scrubbing. Parsnips—another sweet winter vegetable—or parsnips mixed with carrots are also delicious cooked this way.

Serves 4 to 6

1 ½ LBS CARROTS, SCRUBBED
    OR PEELED

1 TBSP BUTTER

1 TBSP HONEY OR BROWN
    SUGAR

1 TSP DIJON MUSTARD

SALT AND FRESHLY GROUND
    BLACK PEPPER

CHOPPED PARSLEY

Cut the carrots into 3-inch lengths and halve or quarter the thicker ends so that they'll cook evenly. Steam or simmer in salted water until tender.

Melt the butter in a medium skillet with the honey, then stir in the mustard and carrots and season with salt and plenty of pepper. Cook over medium heat for several minutes until well coated and bubbling, then toss with chopped parsley and serve.

Because carrots are so sweet, they take well to strong, even aggressive flavors—the sharpness of vinegar, pungent mustards, chile, and sauces whose seasonings are fairly complex. One of my favorites is the Moroccan chermoula, a green sauce based on cilantro, parsley, and garlic, pounded in a mortar, then made a bit rusty with the addition of paprika, cumin, and cayenne. Olive oil binds the flavors and lemon juice gives it that acidic lift. It's delicious with carrots.

Monday

14

St. Valentine's Day

Tuesday

15

Wednesday

16

Thursday

17

Friday

18

Full Moon

Saturday

19

Sunday

20

FEBRUARY

S	M	T	W	T	F	S
		1	2	3	4	5
6	7	8	9	10	11	12
13	14	15	16	17	18	19
20	21	22	23	24	25	26
27	28					

MARCH

S	M	T	W	T	F	S
		1	2	3	4	5
6	7	8	9	10	11	12
13	14	15	16	17	18	19
20	21	22	23	24	25	26
27	28	29	30	31		

FEBRUARY

Monday
21

Presidents' Day (US)

Tuesday
22

Wednesday
23

Thursday
24

Friday
25

Saturday
26

Sunday
27

FEBRUARY

S	M	T	W	T	F	S
		1	2	3	4	5
6	7	8	9	10	11	12
13	14	15	16	17	18	19
20	21	22	23	24	25	26
27	28					

MARCH

S	M	T	W	T	F	S
		1	2	3	4	5
6	7	8	9	10	11	12
13	14	15	16	17	18	19
20	21	22	23	24	25	26
27	28	29	30	31		

Baked Spaghetti Squash with Gruyère and Parsley

A SIMPLE AND VERY SATISFYING combination of flavors. Be sure to puncture the squash in at least a few places before baking, or it will explode in the oven and make a truly amazing mess. Even when properly cooked, the strands of squash will be a little crunchy.

Serves 4

1 SPAGHETTI SQUASH,
    ABOUT 3 LBS

¹/₄ CUP PARSLEY, CHOPPED
    WITH 1 GARLIC CLOVE

1 CUP GRATED GRUYÈRE
    CHEESE

2 TO 4 TBSPS BUTTER

SALT AND FRESHLY GROUND
    BLACK PEPPER

Preheat the oven to 375 and prick the squash in several places with a fork. Bake the squash until the flesh is yielding and soft, an hour or more. When cool enough to handle, slice the squash in half and scrape out the seeds. Drag a fork through the flesh, pulling the strands apart. Toss strands with the parsley, cheese, and butter. Season with salt and pepper.

Tomato sauces of all kinds are also good with spaghetti squash. Toss the strands lightly with olive oil, salt, and pepper, then pile them on a platter. Make a nest in the middle for 1 to 2 cups tomato sauce. Toss, then serve.

Monday   28

Tuesday   1

Wednesday   2

Thursday   3

Friday   4

Saturday   5

Sunday   6

FEBRUARY

S	M	T	W	T	F	S
		1	2	3	4	5
6	7	8	9	10	11	12
13	14	15	16	17	18	19
20	21	22	23	24	25	26
27	28					

MARCH

S	M	T	W	T	F	S
		1	2	3	4	5
6	7	8	9	10	11	12
13	14	15	16	17	18	19
20	21	22	23	24	25	26
27	28	29	30	31		

MARCH

Monday 7

Tuesday 8

Wednesday 9

Ash Wednesday

Thursday 10

MARCH

S	M	T	W	T	F	S
		1	2	3	4	5
6	7	8	9	10	11	12
13	14	15	16	17	18	19
20	21	22	23	24	25	26
27	28	29	30	31		

APRIL

S	M	T	W	T	F	S
					1	2
3	4	5	6	7	8	9
10	11	12	13	14	15	16
17	18	19	20	21	22	23
24	25	26	27	28	29	30

Friday 11

Saturday 12

Sunday 13

Daylight Saving Time Begins

Cauliflower Salad with Green Olives and Capers

PEOPLE ALWAYS LOVE this salad as the dressing has strong, lively flavors. The real secret to making it shine is to slice the cauliflower as thinly as possible.

Serves 4

1 SMALL, FIRM HEAD CAULI-
FLOWER OR BROCCOFLOWER,
ABOUT 12 OZS

2 CUPS WATERCRESS OR INNER
ESCAROLE LEAVES

1 HARD-COOKED EGG, WHITE
AND YOLK SEPARATED

SHERRY VINAIGRETTE
(SEE RIGHT)

2 SCALLIONS, INCLUDING AN
INCH OF GREEN, THINLY
SLICED

1 CUP DICED CELERY HEART
WITH THE LEAVES

1 SMALL GREEN BELL PEPPER,
THINLY SLICED

1 SMALL CUCUMBER, PEELED,
SEEDED, AND CHOPPED

12 PIMIENTO-STUFFED
SPANISH GREEN OLIVES,
HALVED

1 TBSP CAPERS, RINSED

$^1/_2$ CUP PARSLEY LEAVES

Slice off very thin slabs of cauliflower, working your way around the head. Be sure to include the stalk, too, peeled and thinly sliced. Remove the large stems from the watercress and coarsely chop the rest. If you're using escarole, select the pale inner leaves and tear or cut them into small pieces.

Dice the egg white and toss it with the vegetables and greens, olives, capers, and parsley. Add the Sherry Vinaigrette (see below) and toss again.

Sherry Vinaigrette: Pound 1 or 2 cloves of garlic in a mortar with $^1/_4$ teaspoon salt and a hard-cooked egg yolk until it forms a paste. Combine the paste with 1 $^1/_2$ tablespoons sherry vinegar or aged red wine vinegar and 1 teaspoon Dijon mustard in a small bowl, then whisk in 6 tablespoons extra-virgin olive oil and season to taste with pepper.

Skillet Asparagus

CELEBRATE THE FIRST ASPARAGUS OF THE YEAR with your finest extra-virgin olive oil, pure butter, and maybe a fresh spring herb, such as tarragon, chervil, or a few hothouse basil leaves.

Serves 4 to 6

2 TO 3 LBS ASPARAGUS, TRIMMED

SALT AND FRESHLY GROUND BLACK PEPPER

3 TO 6 TBSPS UNSALTED BUTTER
OR EXTRA-VIRGIN OLIVE OIL

2 TBSPS FINELY CHOPPED HERBS, SUCH AS TARRAGON, CHERVIL, OR BASIL

Put the asparagus in a large skillet of cold water with the tips going in the same direction. Bring to a boil, add salt to taste, and simmer uncovered until just tender when pierced with a knife, 8 to 10 minutes. Set the cooked asparagus on a kitchen towel to drain, blot dry, then transfer to a large platter. Dot with butter or drizzle with olive oil, season with pepper, and scatter the herbs over. Gently roll the stalks around to coat them.

After the shine of the new crop is off, roasting asparagus in a hot oven gives it a robust flavor and is convenient when stovetop space is unavailable.

Monday   **14**

Tuesday   **15**

Wednesday   **16**

Thursday   **17**

St. Patrick's Day

Friday   **18**

MARCH

S	M	T	W	T	F	S
		1	2	3	4	5
6	7	8	9	10	11	12
13	14	15	16	17	18	19
20	21	22	23	24	25	26
27	28	29	30	31		

APRIL

S	M	T	W	T	F	S
					1	2
3	4	5	6	7	8	9
10	11	12	13	14	15	16
17	18	19	20	21	22	23
24	25	26	27	28	29	30

Saturday   **19**   **Sunday**   **20**

Full Moon   *First Day of Spring*

MARCH

Monday   **21**

Tuesday   **22**

Wednesday   **23**

Thursday   **24**

MARCH

S	M	T	W	T	F	S
		1	2	3	4	5
6	7	8	9	10	11	12
13	14	15	16	17	18	19
20	21	22	23	24	25	26
27	28	29	30	31		

Friday   **25**

APRIL

S	M	T	W	T	F	S
					1	2
3	4	5	6	7	8	9
10	11	12	13	14	15	16
17	18	19	20	21	22	23
24	25	26	27	28	29	30

Saturday   **26**   Sunday   **27**

Linguine with Asparagus, Lemon, and Spring Herbs

A MINIMAL BUT TRUE PASTA PRIMAVERA. Should they come your way, stew a handful of peas or fava beans with the scallions, as well. This dish can be made entirely with butter or olive oil or a mixture.

Serves 4 to 6

2 TBSPS OLIVE OIL

2 TBSPS BUTTER

1 LARGE BUNCH SCALLIONS, INCLUDING HALF OF THE GREENS, THINLY SLICED

2 $^1/_2$ TSPS GRATED LEMON ZEST

1 TBSP FINELY CHOPPED THYME, SAGE, OR TARRAGON

SALT AND FRESHLY GROUND BLACK PEPPER

2 LBS ASPARAGUS, ROUGH ENDS TRIMMED

1 LB LINGUINE

4 TBSPS PINE NUTS, TOASTED IN A SMALL SKILLET

3 TBSPS CHOPPED PARSLEY

2 TBSPS SNIPPED CHIVES, PLUS BLOSSOMS IF AVAILABLE

FRESHLY GRATED PARMESAN, OPTIONAL

While water is heating for pasta, heat half the oil and butter in a wide skillet over low heat. Add the scallions, lemon zest, thyme, and a few pinches salt and cook slowly, stirring occasionally.

Meanwhile, slice 3-inch tips off the asparagus, then slice the remaining stalks diagonally. When the water boils, salt it, add the asparagus, and cook until partially tender, 3 to 4 minutes. Scoop out asparagus and add it to the scallion mixture. Cook the pasta, then add it to the skillet with some of the water clinging to the strands. Raise the heat and stir in remaining oil, pine nuts, parsley, chives, pepper to taste, and a few tablespoons grated cheese, if using. Divide among pasta plates, grate a little more cheese over each portion, and garnish with chive blossoms.

....

When shopping for asparagus, buy as much as you can afford—people like it and most can easily eat $^1/_2$ pound if given the chance, especially when it's the first of the season. Allow at least 10 thin or 5–6 thick stalks per person.

Monday **28**

Tuesday **29**

Wednesday **30**

Thursday **31**

MARCH

S	M	T	W	T	F	S
		1	2	3	4	5
6	7	8	9	10	11	12
13	14	15	16	17	18	19
20	21	22	23	24	25	26
27	28	29	30	31		

Friday **1**

APRIL

S	M	T	W	T	F	S
					1	2
3	4	5	6	7	8	9
10	11	12	13	14	15	16
17	18	19	20	21	22	23
24	25	26	27	28	29	30

Saturday **2**

Sunday **3**

APRIL

Monday
4

Tuesday
5

Wednesday
6

Thursday
7

Friday
8

Saturday
9

Sunday
10

Baby Artichoke and Scallion Sauté

THESE ARTICHOKES can stand alone, but there's no reason you can't toss them with pasta, stir them into a risotto, or spoon them over garlic-rubbed toast.

Serves 4 to 6

20 TO 24 BABY ARTICHOKES

JUICE OF 2 LEMONS

4 TBSPS WHITE WINE VINEGAR OR ADDITIONAL LEMON JUICE

2 TBSPS EXTRA-VIRGIN OLIVE OIL

1 BUNCH SCALLIONS, INCLUDING AN INCH OF GREEN, THICKLY SLICED

1/2 CUP DRY WHITE WINE

GREMOLATA (3 TBSPS PARSLEY LEAVES CHOPPED WITH 1 GARLIC CLOVE AND 2 TSPS LEMON ZEST)

1 TBSP CHOPPED TARRAGON

SALT AND FRESHLY GROUND BLACK PEPPER

Trim the artichokes, snapping off the tough outer leaves until you get to the pale, inner leaves. As you work, drop them in a bowl of water to cover mixed with the juice of two lemons. When all are done, blanch them in boiling, salted water acidulated with 4 tablespoons white wine vinegar or more lemon juice. Simmer until tender-firm, about 10 minutes, then drain. Halve cooked artichokes lengthwise. (This can be done before finishing the dish.)

Heat the olive oil in a large skillet over high heat. Add the artichokes and sauté until they begin to color in places, then add the scallions and wine. When the wine boils off, add 1 cup water and half the gremolata and tarragon. Lower the heat and simmer until the artichokes are fully tender, 5 to 10 minutes more, then add the remaining gremolata and tarragon and season with salt and pepper. Tip the vegetables, with their juices, onto a serving plate.

The preparation for baby artichokes goes easily and quickly. If they're not available, use 4–6 medium artichokes, leaves trimmed, quartered, the fuzzy choke removed, and the hearts thinly sliced.

Fried Fennel

SERVE THIS as a springtime first course with a wedge of lemon, Garlic Mayonnaise (see below), salsa verde, or Romesco Sauce.

Serves 4 to 6

3 FENNEL BULBS, TRIMMED, ROOT ENDS INTACT

1 EGG BEATEN WITH 1 TBSP MILK

1 CUP FINE FRESH BREAD CRUMBS

OLIVE OIL FOR FRYING

SALT AND FRESHLY GROUND BLACK PEPPER

LEMON WEDGES, OPTIONAL

Slice the fennel lengthwise about $^3/_8$ inch thick. Make sure the pieces are joined at the root. Steam until partially tender, about 10 minutes, then remove. Dip the steamed fennel into the egg mixture, then into bread crumbs. (If you don't wish to use eggs, dredge the fennel in flour.) Heat enough oil in a wide skillet to cover generously. When hot, add the fennel in a single layer and lower the heat to medium. Cook on both sides until golden brown. Season with salt and pepper and serve with lemon wedges or one of the suggested sauces.

Garlic Mayonnaise is especially good with the Fried Fennel. Pound fresh garlic, free of blemishes and sprouts, as many as 4 to 6 cloves, in a mortar with a few pinches salt until a smooth paste forms, which will happen fairly quickly. Stir the paste into 1 cup homemade mayonnaise. Taste and add a little fresh lemon juice if needed for tartness. Stir in a small amount of very hot water to thin the mayonnaise to the consistency of a thick sauce.

Monday   **11**

Tuesday   **12**

Wednesday   **13**

Thursday   **14**

Friday   **15**

Saturday   **16**

Sunday   **17**

Palm Sunday

Full Moon

APRIL

S	M	T	W	T	F	S
					1	2
3	4	5	6	7	8	9
10	11	12	13	14	15	16
17	18	19	20	21	22	23
24	25	26	27	28	29	30

MAY

S	M	T	W	T	F	S
1	2	3	4	5	6	7
8	9	10	11	12	13	14
15	16	17	18	19	20	21
22	23	24	25	26	27	28
29	30	31				

APRIL

Monday   **18**

Passover (Begins at Sundown)

Tuesday   **19**

Wednesday   **20**

Thursday   **21**

APRIL

S	M	T	W	T	F	S
					1	2
3	4	5	6	7	8	9
10	11	12	13	14	15	16
17	18	19	20	21	22	23
24	25	26	27	28	29	30

Friday   **22**

Good Friday

Earth Day

MAY

S	M	T	W	T	F	S
1	2	3	4	5	6	7
8	9	10	11	12	13	14
15	16	17	18	19	20	21
22	23	24	25	26	27	28
29	30	31				

Saturday   **23**   **Sunday**   **24**

Easter

Orthodox Easter

Chard Soup with Sorrel

LIGHT-BODIED BUT ROUNDLY FLAVORED, this is a good soup to begin a large meal. It's quickly made and needs no stock. Chard is available year-round, sorrel mainly in spring. If you can't get sorrel, use fresh lemon juice to give the soup its tart accent. The bright, lemony tartness of sorrel leaves is good with both eggs and vegetables.

Serves 4 to 6

2 TBSPS BUTTER

1 ONION OR 2 MEDIUM LEEKS,
    WHITE PARTS ONLY,
    CHOPPED

3 RED POTATOES, PEELED AND
    THINLY SLICED

1 BUNCH CHARD, STEMS
    REMOVED, ABOUT 10 CUPS
    LEAVES

2 CUPS SORREL LEAVES, STEMS
    REMOVED, OR JUICE OF
    1 LARGE LEMON

SALT AND FRESHLY GROUND
    BLACK PEPPER

$^1/_3$ CUP CRÈME FRAÎCHE OR
    SOUR CREAM

$^1/_2$ CUP COOKED RICE OR
    SMALL TOASTED CROUTONS

Heat the butter in a soup pot over medium-high heat. Add the onion and potatoes and cook, stirring occasionally, until they begin to color, about 8 minutes. Add $^1/_2$ cup water and scrape the bottom of the pot to release any juices that have accumulated. Add the greens and 1 $^1/_2$ teaspoons salt. As soon as they wilt down, after 5 minutes or so, add 6 $^1/_2$ cups water. Bring to a boil, then lower the heat and simmer, partially covered, for 12 to 15 minutes.

Puree the soup, then return it to the pot. Taste for salt and season with pepper. If you didn't use the sorrel, now is the time to add the lemon juice. Mix the crème fraîche with some of the soup to smooth it out, then swirl it back into the soup. Serve with rice or croutons in each bowl.

Sorrel is a perennial herb with soft, tender leaves that look mild but are, in fact, quite tart, which is what makes sorrel so interesting. It wakes up the palate, especially when encountered fresh in a salad. When cooked, the bright green color fades to a dull army green within moments and the tender leaves, minus their stems, fall into a puree. You might get only a few spoon-fuls for a cup of densely packed leaves, but a little goes a long way to enliven a soup—try it in one made with potatoes—or an omelet. If you have a sorrel plant, you'll find this is a very good use for it.

Stir-Fried Peas with Sichuan Pepper Salt

THE SPICY, AROMATIC SALT (below) is delicious with peas, but you can also use plain sea salt. I like my sugar snap peas plump and whole, but you can slice them diagonally to give the dish a more dynamic play of shapes.

Serves 4 to 6

1 ¹/₂ TBSPS ROASTED PEANUT
   OIL

1 GARLIC CLOVE, CHOPPED

1 LB SUGAR SNAP PEAS,
   STRUNG

¹/₂ TO 1 TSP SICHUAN PEPPER
   SALT, OR SEA SALT, TO
   TASTE

Heat a wok or large skillet, then dribble in the oil. When the oil is hot, add the garlic and stir-fry for 30 seconds. Add the peas and stir-fry until they turn bright green. Turn off the heat, sprinkle with the salt, toss again, and serve.

Sichuan Pepper Salt is a delicious condiment for green vegetables, including raw cabbage, asparagus, and also Asian pears. It shines especially on sweet corn and eggs. To make it, simply toast 2 tablespoons Sichuan peppercorns, 1 tablespoon black peppercorns, and ¹/₄ cup sea salt or kosher salt in a heavy, dry skillet until the peppercorns are fragrant and the salt lightly colored. Then grind in a spice grinder or pound in a mortar, using a sieve to remove the peppercorn hulls.

Monday 25

Easter Monday (Canada & UK)

Tuesday 26

Wednesday 27

Thursday 28

APRIL

S	M	T	W	T	F	S
					1	2
3	4	5	6	7	8	9
10	11	12	13	14	15	16
17	18	19	20	21	22	23
24	25	26	27	28	29	30

MAY

S	M	T	W	T	F	S
1	2	3	4	5	6	7
8	9	10	11	12	13	14
15	16	17	18	19	20	21
22	23	24	25	26	27	28
29	30	31				

Friday 29

Saturday 30

Sunday 1

MAY

Monday   2

Early May Bank Holiday (UK)

Tuesday   3

Wednesday   4

Thursday   5

Friday   6

MAY						
S	M	T	W	T	F	S
1	2	3	4	5	6	7
8	9	10	11	12	13	14
15	16	17	18	19	20	21
22	23	24	25	26	27	28
29	30	31				

JUNE						
S	M	T	W	T	F	S
			1	2	3	4
5	6	7	8	9	10	11
12	13	14	15	16	17	18
19	20	21	22	23	24	25
26	27	28	29	30		

Saturday   7   Sunday   8

Mother's Day

Spring Vegetable Stew

COOKING THE VEGETABLES SEPARATELY, then combining them, makes it possible to have everything ready in advance. Radishes and broccoli stems though surprising, give this dish an exceedingly fresh spring look.

Serves 4

SALT AND FRESHLY GROUND
  BLACK PEPPER

12 BABY CARROTS, OR
  2 CARROTS PEELED AND
  THINLY SLICED

$^{1}/_{2}$ CUP SNOW PEAS

6 RADISHES, INCLUDING
  $^{1}/_{2}$ INCH OF THE STEMS,
  HALVED

18 3-INCH ASPARAGUS TIPS

6 SCALLIONS, INCLUDING
  GREENS, CUT INTO 3-INCH
  LENGTHS

2 BROCCOLI STEMS, PEELED
  AND THICKLY SLICED
  DIAGONALLY

4 SMALL TURNIPS, OR
  2 RUTABAGAS AND 2
  TURNIPS, PEELED AND CUT
  INTO SIXTHS

2 TO 4 TBSPS BUTTER

4 THYME SPRIGS, PREFERABLY
  LEMON THYME

1 TBSP FRESH LEMON JUICE

10 SORREL LEAVES, SLICED
  INTO RIBBONS

1 TBSP SNIPPED CHIVES

2 TSPS FINELY CHOPPED
  PARSLEY

1 TSP CHOPPED TARRAGON

Bring 3 quarts of water to a boil and add 1 tablespoon salt. Blanch each kind of vegetable one at a time until barely tender, then remove to a bowl of cold water to stop the cooking. When all are blanched, reserve 1 cup of the cooking water and drain the vegetables. (This can be done ahead of time.)

In a wide skillet, melt the butter with the thyme sprigs. Add the reserved liquid then the vegetables and simmer until they're warmed through. Add the lemon juice and season with salt and pepper. Add the sorrel and herbs and cook for 1 minute more. Serve at once.

While popovers or fresh herb noodles are good accompaniments, I sometimes add some potato gnocchi or cheese tortellini at the end for a soft and surprising mouthful.

Monday

9

Tuesday

10

Wednesday

11

Thursday

12

MAY

S	M	T	W	T	F	S
1	2	3	4	5	6	7
8	9	10	11	12	13	14
15	16	17	18	19	20	21
22	23	24	25	26	27	28
29	30	31				

Friday

13

JUNE

S	M	T	W	T	F	S
			1	2	3	4
5	6	7	8	9	10	11
12	13	14	15	16	17	18
19	20	21	22	23	24	25
26	27	28	29	30		

Saturday

14

Sunday

15

MAY

Monday   **16**

Tuesday   **17**

Full Moon

Wednesday   **18**

Thursday   **19**

MAY

S	M	T	W	T	F	S
1	2	3	4	5	6	7
8	9	10	11	12	13	14
15	16	17	18	19	20	21
22	23	24	25	26	27	28
29	30	31				

Friday   **20**

JUNE

S	M	T	W	T	F	S
			1	2	3	4
5	6	7	8	9	10	11
12	13	14	15	16	17	18
19	20	21	22	23	24	25
26	27	28	29	30		

Saturday   **21**   Sunday   **22**

Fava Beans with Yogurt, Lemon, and Dill

INCREASINGLY AVAILABLE at Italian, Mexican, and farmers' markets, fava beans are a springtime favorite with chefs and are a beautiful seasonal addition to all sorts of spring vegetable stews and pasta dishes.

Serves 4

4 LBS FRESH FAVA BEANS IN
   THEIR PODS

2 ¹/₂ TBSPS EXTRA-VIRGIN
   OLIVE OIL

3 SCALLIONS, INCLUDING
   SOME OF THE GREEN,
   THINLY SLICED

1 TSP FINELY GRATED LEMON
   ZEST

1 TBSP FRESH LEMON JUICE

SALT AND FRESHLY GROUND
   BLACK PEPPER

3 TBSPS FINELY CHOPPED DILL

¹/₃ CUP YOGURT, WHISKED
   UNTIL SMOOTH

Shell the beans, and if large, blanch, then peel them (see below). Cook them in a medium skillet over medium heat in 1 tablespoon of olive oil and 1 cup water until tender, about 10 minutes, then stir in scallions and remove from heat. Whisk together remaining oil, lemon zest and juice, and a pinch of salt. Pour mixture over the beans, add most of the dill, and gently mix. Season with pepper.

Pile the beans in a dish, drizzle yogurt over all, and garnish with remaining dill. Serve warm or chilled.

Getting to the actual beans is sometimes a challenge. Long green pods surround the beans, which are further encased in a skin. When the beans are young (about the size of a thumbnail), this skin needn't be removed; however, it's rather tough on more mature beans. To remove, blanch the beans for one minute in boiling water, drain, and pinch off the skins with your fingers. One pound of pods yields roughly ¹/₂ cup of shelled beans.

Bright Green Spinach and Pea Soup

BRIEF COOKING preserves this utterly simple soup's vivid green. The color lasts only about 10 minutes, so organize yourself to serve the soup right away!

Serves 4 to 6

2 TBSPS OLIVE OIL, BUTTER, OR A MIXTURE

2 BUNCHES SCALLIONS, INCLUDING HALF THE GREENS, CHOPPED

1 SMALL ONION, THINLY SLICED

3 CARROTS, THINLY SLICED

1 CELERY RIB, THINLY SLICED

1 TBSP CHOPPED MARJORAM OR BASIL OR 1 TSP DRIED

SALT AND FRESHLY GROUND BLACK PEPPER

10 PARSLEY SPRIGS, CHOPPED

1 LARGE BUNCH SPINACH, STEMS REMOVED

1 CUP PEAS, FRESH OR FROZEN

LEMON JUICE TO TASTE

FOR GARNISH: CRÈME FRAÎCHE, SMALL TOASTED CROUTONS, CALENDULA PETALS

Warm the oil in a soup pot and add the scallions, onion, carrots, celery, herbs, 1 teaspoon salt, and $1/2$ cup water. Cover and stew for 5 minutes, then add 5 $1/2$ cups water and bring to a boil. Lower the heat and simmer, uncovered, for 20 minutes. Add the spinach and peas. Poke the spinach leaves into the soup and cook until they turn a bright green, 2 to 3 minutes. Remove from the heat and blend the soup in two batches until smooth. Taste for salt, season with pepper, and stir in enough lemon juice, starting with $1/2$ teaspoon, to bring up the flavors. Serve immediately with a swirl of crème fraîche, the croutons, and blossoms floating on top.

....

Edible flowers, such as calendula petals, borage, hyssop, marigold, or nasturtium flowers make a cheerful garnish. My own preference is for those blossoms that contribute flavor or are an obvious part of the plant to use, such as arugula or sage that's in bloom. Choose unsprayed garden blooms and shake them gently to knock out any small insects. Float or swish them back and forth in a bowl of water, then shake dry. Separate those that grow in a cluster at the base, like chive blossoms. Pluck off petals of flowers like calendulas or marigolds.

Monday **23**

Victoria Day (Canada)

Tuesday **24**

Wednesday **25**

Thursday **26**

MAY

S	M	T	W	T	F	S
1	2	3	4	5	6	7
8	9	10	11	12	13	14
15	16	17	18	19	20	21
22	23	24	25	26	27	28
29	30	31				

Friday **27**

JUNE

S	M	T	W	T	F	S
			1	2	3	4
5	6	7	8	9	10	11
12	13	14	15	16	17	18
19	20	21	22	23	24	25
26	27	28	29	30		

Saturday **28**

Sunday **29**

MAY / JUNE

Monday   30

Memorial Day (US)

Spring Bank Holiday (UK)

Tuesday   31

Wednesday   1

Thursday   2

MAY						
S	M	T	W	T	F	S
1	2	3	4	5	6	7
8	9	10	11	12	13	14
15	16	17	18	19	20	21
22	23	24	25	26	27	28
29	30	31				

Friday   3

JUNE						
S	M	T	W	T	F	S
			1	2	3	4
5	6	7	8	9	10	11
12	13	14	15	16	17	18
19	20	21	22	23	24	25
26	27	28	29	30		

Saturday   4   Sunday   5

Warm Green Bean Salad

LITTLE GREEN BEANS, yellow wax, or wide Romano beans tossed warm with a vinaigrette make a stellar summer salad. If you want to mix varieties, boil each type separately so that they each cook perfectly.

Serves 4

1 1/2 LBS SLENDER GREEN, YELLOW WAX, OR ROMANO BEANS

SALT

3 TO 4 TBSPS EXTRA-VIRGIN OLIVE OIL AS NEEDED

1 TBSP FRESH LEMON JUICE, TO TASTE

CHOPPED HERBS, SUCH AS PARSLEY, CHERVIL, BASIL, OR TARRAGON

Tip and tail the beans. Boil the beans in plenty of salted water, uncovered. Drain, or scoop them out, while they're still a little on the firm side. Shake off the excess water, then lay them on a clean kitchen towel to dry for a few minutes. Toss the warm beans with enough oil to coat well, then add the lemon juice and herbs. Serve immediately—if you plan to serve them later, either dress them just before serving or add the acid at the last minute to keep their color intact.

In addition to good olive oil and fresh lemon juice, many vinaigrettes complement summer bush and pole beans, including those made with walnut oil as well as olive oil. Other sauces that make good companions include a classic pesto, salsa verdes of all kinds, and a rustic tapenade based on chopped olives, capers, and garlic. Herb butters are also good tossed with the warm beans, though less salad like without the vinegar. Speaking of herbs, fresh beans go with a quite a few, such as basil, dill, lemon thyme, lovage, parsley, and tarragon.

Monday

6

Tuesday

7

Wednesday

8

Thursday

9

Friday

10

Saturday

11

Sunday

12

JUNE

S	M	T	W	T	F	S
			1	2	3	4
5	6	7	8	9	10	11
12	13	14	15	16	17	18
19	20	21	22	23	24	25
26	27	28	29	30		

JULY

S	M	T	W	T	F	S
					1	2
3	4	5	6	7	8	9
10	11	12	13	14	15	16
17	18	19	20	21	22	23
24	25	26	27	28	29	30
31						

JUNE

Monday
13

Tuesday
14

Wednesday
15

Full Moon

Thursday
16

Friday
17

Saturday
18

Sunday
19

Father's Day

Linguine with Onions, Peas, and Basil

NEW ONIONS FROM THE GARDEN and fresh peas make a delicate dish for late spring or early summer. Butter and olive oil are both good with peas—although I prefer butter here.

Serves 2 to 4

2 TBSPS BUTTER

1 RED ONION, QUARTERED AND THINLY SLICED CROSSWISE

1 ½ LBS FRESH PEAS, SHUCKED, OR 2 CUPS FROZEN

SALT AND FRESHLY GROUND WHITE PEPPER

8 OZS FRESH OR DRIED LINGUINE

¼ CUP SMALL BASIL LEAVES, PLUCKED INTO PIECES

3 TBSPS FRESHLY GRATED PARMESAN

Start heating a large pot of water for the pasta. Meanwhile, melt 1 tablespoon of the butter in a wide skillet. Add the onion and a few spoonfuls of water and stew over low heat until the onions are soft, 8 to 10 minutes. Add the peas and cook until they're bright green and tender, a minute or two. Season with salt and a little pepper.

Cook the pasta in the boiling, salted water, then scoop it out and add it to the peas, allowing a little water to fall into the pan. Add the basil and remaining butter, then toss with a large fork and spoon. Distribute the pasta among heated plates, then go back for the peas that have stayed behind and spoon them over the pasta. Add a dusting of Parmesan to each plate.

Grilling is another delicious way to prepare summer's onions. Peel and slice large onions into ½-inch-thick rounds and skewer them with 1 or 2 toothpicks to prevent the rings from separating. Brush both sides with olive oil and season with salt and pepper. Grill for 8 to 10 minutes, until they're nicely marked and softened. Serve with butter or olive oil and lots of freshly ground pepper, with a splash of your favorite vinegar, herb butter, or green herb sauce.

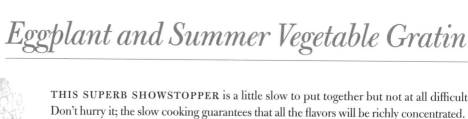

Eggplant and Summer Vegetable Gratin

THIS SUPERB SHOWSTOPPER is a little slow to put together but not at all difficult. Don't hurry it; the slow cooking guarantees that all the flavors will be richly concentrated.

Serves 4 to 6

2 ¹/₂ LBS GLOBE EGGPLANT (PREFERABLY ON THE SMALL SIDE)

OLIVE OIL

SALT AND FRESHLY GROUND BLACK PEPPER

2 LARGE ONIONS, FINELY DICED

3 GARLIC CLOVES, CHOPPED

1 LARGE RED BELL PEPPER, FINELY DICED

2 LARGE RIPE TOMATOES, PEELED, SEEDED, AND CHOPPED

10 LARGE BASIL LEAVES, TORN INTO SMALL PIECES

1 CUP FRESH BREAD CRUMBS FROM STURDY WHITE BREAD

¹/₄ CUP FRESHLY GRATED PARMESAN

Preheat the oven to 425. Slice the eggplant into ¹/₂-inch-thick rounds. If the eggplant is very fresh, there's no need to salt it. Otherwise, sprinkle with salt, let stand 30 minutes, then blot dry. Brush both sides of each round with oil and bake on a sheet pan until browned and tender on both sides, about 25 minutes. Season with salt and pepper and set aside. Reduce the oven temperature to 325.

Heat 3 tablespoons olive oil in a wide skillet, add the onions and garlic, and cook over medium heat, about 8 minutes. Raise the heat a little, add the pepper and tomatoes, and continue cooking, stirring occasionally, until everything is soft and thickened to a jam, about 20 minutes. Raise the temperature at the end to reduce the juices. Add the basil and season to taste with salt and pepper.

Lightly oil a 2 ¹/₂-quart gratin dish. Make a layer of eggplant in the bottom and spread a third of the tomato-onion sauce on top, followed by another layer of eggplant, half the remaining sauce, then the rest of the eggplant. End with the remaining sauce on top. Cover the dish and bake for 45 minutes. Toss the bread crumbs with olive oil to moisten and the grated cheese. Remove the cover, add bread crumbs and cheese, raise the oven temperature to 375, and bake until the crumbs are nicely browned and crisp on top, about 25 minutes.

Monday 20

Tuesday 21

First Day of Summer

Wednesday 22

Thursday 23

JUNE						
S	M	T	W	T	F	S
			1	2	3	4
5	6	7	8	9	10	11
12	13	14	15	16	17	18
19	20	21	22	23	24	25
26	27	28	29	30		

Friday 24

JULY						
S	M	T	W	T	F	S
					1	2
3	4	5	6	7	8	9
10	11	12	13	14	15	16
17	18	19	20	21	22	23
24	25	26	27	28	29	30
31						

Saturday 25

Sunday 26

JUNE / JULY

Monday 27

Tuesday 28

Wednesday 29

Thursday 30

Friday 1

Canada Day

Saturday 2

Sunday 3

JUNE

S	M	T	W	T	F	S
			1	2	3	4
5	6	7	8	9	10	11
12	13	14	15	16	17	18
19	20	21	22	23	24	25
26	27	28	29	30		

JULY

S	M	T	W	T	F	S
					1	2
3	4	5	6	7	8	9
10	11	12	13	14	15	16
17	18	19	20	21	22	23
24	25	26	27	28	29	30
31						

Tomato Salads

RIPE SUMMER TOMATOES make some of the best—and easiest—summer salads. They needn't be dressed, although tomatoes that are low in acid benefit from a squeeze of fresh lemon juice or a splash of balsamic vinegar. Remember, tomatoes are best warm from the sun or at least at room temperature.

When it comes to seasonings, many herbs and their perfumed blossoms form a natural alliance with tomatoes: dill and its yellow flowers, marjoram, chives and their purple blossoms, the various thymes, the blue star-shaped borage flowers, violet rosemary blossoms, purple sage, tarragon, and others.

Tomato and Avocado Salad Cut 2 large tomatoes around the equator, remove the seeds, and dice them into large pieces. Toss with 1 avocado, cut in good-sized chunks, and a few chopped scallions, parsley or cilantro, a pinch of salt, and freshly cracked pepper to taste. Squeeze a little lime or lemon juice over all and serve with warm tortillas and queso fresco or feta cheese.

Tomato and Sweet Onion Salad When you can get genuine sweet Vidalia, Walla Walla, or Maui onions, as well as ripe, luscious tomatoes, this is the salad to make. Peel whole onions, then slice them into thin rounds. Slice the tomatoes into rounds. On a platter, overlap layers of onions and tomatoes so that both can easily be picked up at once. Serve right away or chill before serving.

Tomato and Mozzarella Salad The simplicity and clarity of the components are what make *insalata caprese* a classic that never grows tiresome, but its success depends on top-quality ingredients. The tomatoes should have a slightly tart edge to contrast with the mildness of the cheese. Slice fresh mozzarella and ripe but firm tomatoes into rounds and overlap them on a plate. Drizzle extra-virgin olive oil over the top and season with salt and freshly ground pepper. Tear basil leaves over the top or tuck them in between the tomatoes and cheese.

Monday

4

Independence Day (US)

Tuesday

5

Wednesday

6

Thursday

7

Friday

8

Saturday

9

Sunday

10

JULY

S	M	T	W	T	F	S
					1	2
3	4	5	6	7	8	9
10	11	12	13	14	15	16
17	18	19	20	21	22	23
24	25	26	27	28	29	30
31						

AUGUST

S	M	T	W	T	F	S
	1	2	3	4	5	6
7	8	9	10	11	12	13
14	15	16	17	18	19	20
21	22	23	24	25	26	27
28	29	30	31			

JULY

Monday   **11**

Tuesday   **12**

Wednesday   **13**

Thursday   **14**

Friday   **15**

Full Moon

Saturday   **16**   Sunday   **17**

JULY						
S	M	T	W	T	F	S
					1	2
3	4	5	6	7	8	9
10	11	12	13	14	15	16
17	18	19	20	21	22	23
24	25	26	27	28	29	30
31						

AUGUST						
S	M	T	W	T	F	S
	1	2	3	4	5	6
7	8	9	10	11	12	13
14	15	16	17	18	19	20
21	22	23	24	25	26	27
28	29	30	31			

Zucchini and Fresh Herb Fritters

SIMPLY DELICIOUS! Serve these plain or with a dollop of yogurt sauce, salsa verde, or a dollop of Green Chile Mayonnaise (see below). For a vegan version, replace the eggs with $^{1}/_{2}$ cup pureed silken tofu.

Serves 4

SALT AND FRESHLY CRACKED
  BLACK PEPPER

2 LBS GREEN OR GOLDEN
  ZUCCHINI, COARSELY
  GRATED

2 EGGS, BEATEN

1 BUNCH SCALLIONS,
  INCLUDING AN INCH OF
  GREEN, THINLY SLICED

1 CUP DRIED BREAD CRUMBS

2 GARLIC CLOVES, FINELY
  CHOPPED

$^{1}/_{2}$ CUP CHOPPED PARSLEY

1 TBSP CHOPPED MARJORAM
  OR BASIL

OLIVE OIL, AS NEEDED

Lightly salt the zucchini and set it aside in a colander to drain for 30 minutes. Meanwhile, mix the remaining ingredients together except the oil and pepper. Quickly rinse the squash, squeeze out all the excess water, then stir it into the batter. Taste for salt and season with pepper.

Film two large skillets with olive oil. When hot, drop in the batter—$^{1}/_{4}$ cup makes a fritter about 3 $^{1}/_{2}$ inches across—and cook over medium heat until golden on the bottom. Turn and cook the second side. Serve hot with or without Green Chile Mayonnaise.

Green Chile Mayonnaise is a tangy accompaniment to these fresh fritters, easily made by mixing several minced and seeded jalapeño peppers, an unseeded serrano chile (if you like it hot), or a large Anaheim chile, grilled, peeled, seeded, and finely minced, into a cup of homemade mayonnaise.

Corn Pudding Soufflé

THIS PUDDING forms a soufflé's crown but is slower to fall. For a summer dinner serve the pudding accompanied with tomatoes glazed with balsamic vinegar, grilled zucchini, and a side of black beans, and Cilantro Salsa (see below).

Serves 4

3 TBSPS BUTTER, PLUS MORE
    FOR THE DISH

2 CUPS CORN KERNELS,
    PREFERABLY FRESH, FROM
    ABOUT 3 EARS

1 CUP MILK

2 TBSPS FINELY DICED
    SHALLOT OR SCALLION

3 TBSPS FLOUR

$^1/_2$ CUP CRUMBLED GOAT
    CHEESE, CHEDDAR, OR FETA

SALT AND FRESHLY CRACKED
    WHITE PEPPER

3 EGGS, SEPARATED

CILANTRO SALSA (SEE RIGHT)

Preheat the oven to 375. Butter a 6-cup soufflé dish. Puree 1 $^1/_2$ cups corn with the milk for a full 3 minutes, then pour it into a fine sieve and press out the liquid. Set the liquid aside and discard the solids.

Melt the butter in a saucepan, add the shallot, and cook over heat for 1 minute. Stir in the flour, then whisk in the corn-milk and cook over medium heat, stirring constantly, for 5 minutes. Remove, stir in the remaining corn, cheese, $^1/_2$ teaspoon salt, and a little pepper. Warm the yolks with $^1/_2$ cup of the mixture, then return them to the pan, stirring briskly.

Beat the whites until they hold firm peaks, then fold them into the base. Pour the batter into the dish and set in a baking pan with boiling water to come halfway up the side. Bake until a golden puffy crown has emerged and the pudding is sturdy, about an hour. Serve warm with sauce.

Cilantro Salsa: Finely chop 1 seeded jalapeño chile, 1 large bunch cilantro, $^1/_2$ cup mint leaves, and 2 garlic cloves. Stir in $^1/_4$ cup water, $^1/_2$ cup plus 2 tablespoons extra-virgin olive oil, $^1/_2$ teaspoon ground cumin, $^1/_2$ teaspoon ground coriander, and salt to taste. Made in a blender, the sauce will be thick, creamy, and flecked with green.

Monday 18

Tuesday 19

Wednesday 20

Thursday 21

Friday 22

Saturday 23

Sunday 24

JULY

S	M	T	W	T	F	S
					1	2
3	4	5	6	7	8	9
10	11	12	13	14	15	16
17	18	19	20	21	22	23
24	25	26	27	28	29	30
31						

AUGUST

S	M	T	W	T	F	S
	1	2	3	4	5	6
7	8	9	10	11	12	13
14	15	16	17	18	19	20
21	22	23	24	25	26	27
28	29	30	31			

JULY

Monday   25

Tuesday   26

Wednesday   27

Thursday   28

Friday   29

Saturday   30   Sunday   31

JULY

S	M	T	W	T	F	S
					1	2
3	4	5	6	7	8	9
10	11	12	13	14	15	16
17	18	19	20	21	22	23
24	25	26	27	28	29	30
31						

AUGUST

S	M	T	W	T	F	S
	1	2	3	4	5	6
7	8	9	10	11	12	13
14	15	16	17	18	19	20
21	22	23	24	25	26	27
28	29	30	31			

Simple Summer Stew with Herb Butter

BY CHOOSING from all the new varieties of beans, squash, and tomatoes that appear in the market during the summer, you can create endless variations using this single recipe.

Serves 4

1 ¹/₂ TBSPS EACH CHOPPED
    MARJORAM, BASIL, AND
    PARSLEY

¹/₂ TSP GRATED LEMON ZEST

SALT AND FRESHLY GROUND
    BLACK PEPPER

4 TBSPS BUTTER, SOFTENED

8 OZS GREEN BEANS, PREFER-
    ABLY SKINNY ONES, TIPPED,
    CUT INTO 3-INCH LENGTHS

1 TBSP OLIVE OR SUNFLOWER
    SEED OIL

1 SMALL ONION, FINELY DICED

1 GARLIC CLOVE, THINLY
    SLICED

8 OZS SUMMER SQUASH,
    DICED OR SLICED INTO
    ROUNDS

1 RED OR YELLOW BELL
    PEPPER, CUT INTO SQUARES

1 LARGE TOMATO, PEELED,
    SEEDED, AND DICED

3 CUPS FRESH CORN KERNELS,
    FROM ABOUT 4 EARS

Combine the marjoram, basil, parsley, lemon zest, a pinch of salt, and the butter in a small bowl. Mix thoroughly and set aside.

Bring a pot of water to a boil and add salt. Cook the beans, uncovered, for 2 minutes and then drain.

Heat the oil in a wide pan over high heat with the onion and garlic. Sauté for 1 minute, then add ¹/₂ cup water, lower the heat, cover, and simmer for 5 minutes. Add the cooked beans, squash, pepper, tomato, and corn. Season with ¹/₂ teaspoon salt, cover, and simmer over low heat for 10 minutes or until tender. Stir in as much of the butter as you wish to use, taste for salt, and season with pepper.

To peel a tomato, slash a little X at the base with a knife, then drop it into a pan of boiling water. When you see the edges of the X begin to curl, after 10 to 20 seconds, scoop it out and drop it into a bowl of cold water. The skin can then easily be slipped off.

AUGUST

Monday 1

Tuesday 2

Wednesday 3

Thursday 4

Friday 5

Saturday 6

Sunday 7

AUGUST

S	M	T	W	T	F	S
	1	2	3	4	5	6
7	8	9	10	11	12	13
14	15	16	17	18	19	20
21	22	23	24	25	26	27
28	29	30	31			

SEPTEMBER

S	M	T	W	T	F	S
					1	2	3
4	5	6	7	8	9	10
11	12	13	14	15	16	17
18	19	20	21	22	23	24
25	26	27	28	29	30	

AUGUST

Monday   8

Tuesday   9

Wednesday   10

Thursday   11

Friday   12

Saturday   13   Sunday   14

Full Moon

Watermelon with Mint, Lime, and Feta

A SWEET-SALTY-TART fruit salad that's enormously refreshing—and quite surprising.

Serves 2

1 LB WATERMELON, MORE
  OR LESS

1 TBSP MINT LEAVES, PLUS
  WHOLE SPRIGS FOR
  GARNISH

$^1/_4$ CUP DICED MILD FETA

JUICE OF 1 LIME

SALT AND FRESHLY GROUND
  BLACK PEPPER

Seed the melon and cut into bite-size pieces. Arrange them on plates and sprinkle with the chopped mint and feta. Season with the lime juice, a pinch of salt, and pepper. Serve garnished with mint sprigs.

Feta cheese is made in Greece, France, Israel, Denmark, and elsewhere, but it's also made here at home, too. Look in your farmers' market for cow- or goat-milk feta made in a small dairy near you. Taste it. No matter where it's made or from what kind of milk, feta cheese can vary in saltiness, something to keep in mind when you strew it over your melon. While you're at it, see if your farmers' market has yellow-fleshed watermelons as well as the red-fleshed varieties. If so, give it a try, alone or mixed with the red.

Cold Tomato Soup

THIS SOUP SHOULD BE A STAPLE in everyone's August kitchen. It requires only ripe, juicy tomatoes and time in the refrigerator.

Serves 4 to 6

4 LBS VINE-RIPENED TOMATOES, PEELED AND SEEDED, JUICE RESERVED

SALT AND FRESHLY GROUND BLACK PEPPER

SUGAR AND/OR SHERRY VINEGAR, AS NEEDED

EXTRA-VIRGIN OLIVE OIL OR SOUR CREAM (TO FINISH)

FINELY CHOPPED BASIL OR MARJORAM

2 SCALLIONS, INCLUDING A FEW OF THE GREENS, THINLY SLICED

Chop the tomatoes by hand until they're very fine, almost a puree. (You can use a blender, but it introduces so much air that the tomatoes turn frothy and pink.) Put the tomatoes in a bowl and add the reserved juice and 2 teaspoons salt. Cover and chill well. Taste and add more salt if needed. If the tomatoes are very tart, add 1 teaspoon sugar and a few drops vinegar to balance the flavors.

Ladle the soup into bowls and thread a spoonful of olive oil over the top of each. Add pepper and garnish with the basil and scallions.

So many flavors flatter tomatoes; this soup is easy to tailor to whatever else you happen to be serving and to a multitude of garnishes. Try lightly whipped cream flavored with minced herbs, curry-flavored oil, lemon zest chopped with garlic and parsley or lovage leaves, ribbons of opal basil, cooked rice, or more diced tomatoes of different colors.

Monday **15**

Tuesday **16**

Wednesday **17**

Thursday **18**

Friday **19**

AUGUST

S	M	T	W	T	F	S
	1	2	3	4	5	6
7	8	9	10	11	12	13
14	15	16	17	18	19	20
21	22	23	24	25	26	27
28	29	30	31			

SEPTEMBER

S	M	T	W	T	F	S
				1	2	3
4	5	6	7	8	9	10
11	12	13	14	15	16	17
18	19	20	21	22	23	24
25	26	27	28	29	30	

Saturday **20**

Sunday **21**

AUGUST

Monday 22

Tuesday 23

Wednesday 24

Thursday 25

Friday 26

Saturday 27

Sunday 28

AUGUST

S	M	T	W	T	F	S
	1	2	3	4	5	6
7	8	9	10	11	12	13
14	15	16	17	18	19	20
21	22	23	24	25	26	27
28	29	30	31			

SEPTEMBER

S	M	T	W	T	F	S
				1	2	3
4	5	6	7	8	9	10
11	12	13	14	15	16	17
18	19	20	21	22	23	24
25	26	27	28	29	30	

Corn with Cumin, Chile, and Tomato

TO GET CORN OFF THE COB, hold an ear with one end resting on the counter or in a large bowl. Using a sharp knife and a sawing motion, slice right down the ear, removing the top halves of the kernels. Then reverse your knife and, using the dull side, press it down the length of the ear to push out the rest of the corn and its milk—these are called the *scrapings*.

Serves 4 to 6

6 LARGE EARS CORN, KERNELS
   AND SCRAPINGS REMOVED
   SEPARATELY

1 GARLIC CLOVE

1 TSP GROUND, TOASTED
   CUMIN SEEDS

SALT AND FRESHLY GROUND
   BLACK PEPPER

2 TBSPS BUTTER OR OLIVE OIL

1 ONION, FINELY DICED

1 LONG GREEN ANAHEIM OR
   NEW MEXICAN CHILE,
   ROASTED AND DICED

1 LARGE RIPE TOMATO,
   SEEDED AND DICED

1 TBSP CHOPPED PARSLEY,
   CILANTRO, OR DILL

Puree 1 cup of the corn kernels with 1 cup water in a blender for 3 minutes. Strain, pushing out as much liquid as possible. Discard the solids. Meanwhile, pound the garlic in a mortar with the cumin, $1/2$ teaspoon salt, and a little pepper until smooth. Heat the butter in a wide skillet with the onion, pounded garlic, and chile. Sauté over medium heat for 4 minutes. Stir in the remaining corn kernels, scrapings, and corn milk. Lower the heat, cover the pan, and simmer for 5 minutes. Add the tomato at the end and cook until warmed through. Taste for salt, stir in the parsley, and serve.

For a variation, use tangy feta cheese to temper the sweetness of the corn. Make the dish as directed, then transfer it to a lightly buttered gratin dish. Top with crumbled feta and bake until bubbling and hot, about 25 minutes. Brown under the broiler, then serve.

AUGUST / SEPTEMBER

Monday　29

Summer Bank Holiday (UK)

Tuesday　30

Wednesday　31

Thursday　1

Friday　2

Saturday　3

Sunday　4

AUGUST

S	M	T	W	T	F	S
	1	2	3	4	5	6
7	8	9	10	11	12	13
14	15	16	17	18	19	20
21	22	23	24	25	26	27
28	29	30	31			

SEPTEMBER

S	M	T	W	T	F	S
				1	2	3
4	5	6	7	8	9	10
11	12	13	14	15	16	17
18	19	20	21	22	23	24
25	26	27	28	29	30	

SEPTEMBER

Monday

5

Labor Day (US & Canada)

Tuesday

6

Wednesday

7

Thursday

8

Friday

9

Saturday

10

Sunday

11

SEPTEMBER

S	M	T	W	T	F	S
				1	2	3
4	5	6	7	8	9	10
11	12	13	14	15	16	17
18	19	20	21	22	23	24
25	26	27	28	29	30	

OCTOBER

S	M	T	W	T	F	S
						1
2	3	4	5	6	7	8
9	10	11	12	13	14	15
16	17	18	19	20	21	22
23	24	25	26	27	28	29
30	31					

Fettuccine with Sautéed Peppers and Parsley

COLORFUL AND UNCOMPLICATED, the peppers in this dish echo the shape of the fettuccine.

Serves 4 to 6

4 LARGE BELL PEPPERS—
   RED, YELLOW, ORANGE, OR
   A MIXTURE

3 TBSPS OLIVE OIL

SALT AND FRESHLY GROUND
   BLACK PEPPER

1 LB FETTUCCINE

²/₃ CUP CHOPPED PARSLEY

FRESHLY GRATED PARMESAN,
   OPTIONAL

Start by heating a large pot of water for the pasta. Meanwhile, cut the peppers into strips about as wide as the fettuccine. Heat the oil in a large skillet over high heat, then add the peppers; give a stir, let them sit for a few minutes, and stir again. Continue cooking in this fashion for about 10 minutes. The peppers should caramelize here and there along the edges, soften, and yield their juices but not lose their skins. They'll smell very sweet. Season with salt and pepper, add a ladle of the pasta water, and turn the heat to low.

Add salt to the boiling water and cook the pasta until al dente. Scoop it out and add it to the peppers. Raise the heat and toss the pasta and peppers with the parsley. Serve with Parmesan grated over all, if desired.

For a luscious variation, toss 1 pound rigatoni or other sturdy pasta shape in place of the fettuccine with ¹/₂ cup Garlic or Saffron Mayonnaise (2 large pinches of saffron, ground in a mortar and mixed with 1 tablespoon of boiling water, then stirred into homemade mayonnaise), then add the peppers.

Artichokes Stuffed with Bread Crumbs, Capers, and Herbs

TO MAKE AN ARTICHOKE CONTAINER, steam or boil a whole artichoke, then rinse it under cold water. Reach inside and pull out the cone of inner leaves with a twist of your fingers, then use a spoon to scrape out the choke. Trim the outer leaves if you want a more refined look.

Serves 4

4 ARTICHOKES

1 ³/₄ CUPS FRESH BREAD CRUMBS

¹/₄ CUP EXTRA-VIRGIN OLIVE OIL

2 GARLIC CLOVES, MINCED

3 TBSPS CHOPPED PARSLEY

4 TSPS CHOPPED THYME OR MARJORAM

¹/₂ CUP FRESHLY GRATED PARMESAN OR PECORINO CHEESE

2 TBSPS CHOPPED GREEN OLIVES

2 TBSPS CAPERS, RINSED

1 TO 2 TSPS RED WINE VINEGAR

1 ROMA TOMATO, DICED

SALT AND FRESHLY GROUND BLACK PEPPER

1 LARGE ONION, THINLY SLICED

¹/₄ CUP DRY WHITE WINE OR WATER

Prepare the artichokes as described above. Toss the bread crumbs with half the oil and cook in a skillet over medium heat until crisp and golden. Combine with the garlic, parsley, 1 tablespoon of the thyme, cheese, olives, and capers. Moisten with the vinegar, stir in the tomato, and season with salt and pepper. Pack the mixture firmly into the artichokes.

Preheat the oven to 375. Sauté the onion and remaining thyme in a skillet in the remaining oil over medium heat until softened, 8 to 10 minutes. Season with salt and pepper, then transfer to a baking dish. Place the artichokes on the onions and pour the wine into the dish. Cover with parchment or wax paper, then with aluminum foil. Bake until heated through, about 30 minutes, then remove the cover and brown under the broiler.

These artichokes are delicious with a spoonful of Garlic Mayonnaise.

SEPTEMBER

Monday   **12**

Full Moon

Tuesday   **13**

Wednesday   **14**

Thursday   **15**

SEPTEMBER

S	M	T	W	T	F	S
				1	2	3
4	5	6	7	8	9	10
11	12	13	14	15	16	17
18	19	20	21	22	23	24
25	26	27	28	29	30	

OCTOBER

S	M	T	W	T	F	S
						1
2	3	4	5	6	7	8
9	10	11	12	13	14	15
16	17	18	19	20	21	22
23	24	25	26	27	28	29
30	31					

Friday   **16**

Saturday   **17**

Sunday   **18**

SEPTEMBER

Monday   19

Tuesday   20

Wednesday   21

International Day of Peace

Thursday   22

Friday   23

First Day of Autumn

Saturday   24   Sunday   25

SEPTEMBER

S	M	T	W	T	F	S
				1	2	3
4	5	6	7	8	9	10
11	12	13	14	15	16	17
18	19	20	21	22	23	24
25	26	27	28	29	30	

OCTOBER

S	M	T	W	T	F	S
						1
2	3	4	5	6	7	8
9	10	11	12	13	14	15
16	17	18	19	20	21	22
23	24	25	26	27	28	29
30	31					

Spicy Eggplant Spread

FRAGRANT THAI, ANISE, OR CINNAMON BASIL is an exotic choice in this sweet, spicy puree, but regular basil will also be delicious.

Makes about 2 cups

1 LB EGGPLANT, ANY VARIETY

1 ½ TBSPS LIGHT BROWN
    SUGAR

1 TBSP RICE WINE VINEGAR

1 TBSP MUSHROOM OR DARK
    CHINESE SOY SAUCE

2 TO 3 SERRANO CHILES,
    FINELY MINCED

3 TBSPS DARK SESAME OR
    ROASTED PEANUT OIL

3 GARLIC CLOVES, MINCED

3 TBSPS CHOPPED BASIL

SALT

TOASTED BLACK SESAME
    SEEDS, OPTIONAL

Preheat the oven to 425. Slash the eggplant in several places so it won't explode. Bake until soft to the point of collapsing, 30 to 40 minutes, allowing the skin to char in places to give the dish a smoky flavor. Remove to a colander to cool. Peel—don't worry about stubborn flecks of skin—and coarsely chop the flesh.

Mix the sugar, vinegar, soy sauce, and chiles together. Heat a wok or skillet over high heat and add the oil. When it begins to haze, add the garlic and stir-fry for 30 seconds. Add the eggplant and stir-fry for 2 minutes, then add the sauce and fry for 1 minute more. Remove from the heat and stir in the chopped basil. Taste for seasoning.

Mound the eggplant in a bowl, and garnish with chopped basil or toasted black sesame seeds.

Monday

26

Tuesday

27

Wednesday

28

Rosh Hashanah (Begins at Sundown)

Thursday

29

Friday

30

Saturday

1

Sunday

2

SEPTEMBER

S	M	T	W	T	F	S
					1	2	3
4	5	6	7	8	9	10
11	12	13	14	15	16	17
18	19	20	21	22	23	24
25	26	27	28	29	30	

OCTOBER

S	M	T	W	T	F	S
						1
2	3	4	5	6	7	8
9	10	11	12	13	14	15
16	17	18	19	20	21	22
23	24	25	26	27	28	29
30	31					

OCTOBER

Monday   3

Tuesday   4

Wednesday   5

Thursday   6

Friday   7

Yom Kippur (Begins at Sundown)

Saturday   8   Sunday   9

OCTOBER

S	M	T	W	T	F	S
						1
2	3	4	5	6	7	8
9	10	11	12	13	14	15
16	17	18	19	20	21	22
23	24	25	26	27	28	29
30	31					

NOVEMBER

S	M	T	W	T	F	S
		1	2	3	4	5
6	7	8	9	10	11	12
13	14	15	16	17	18	19
20	21	22	23	24	25	26
27	28	29	30			

It's time to order your 2012

DEBORAH MADISON

Vegetarian Every Day

engagement calendar

Take this form to your book or stationery dealer, or mail to:

UNIVERSE PUBLISHING

300 Park Avenue South

New York, NY 10010

Herewith my check or money order for the 2012 *Vegetarian Every Day* engagement calendar (please make check payable to Universe Publishing):

_____ copies @ $13.99 each   _____

Sales tax where applicable   _____

(Shipments to NY assess applicable local and state sales tax on total merchandise and shipping charge)

Postage/handling (Continental U.S. only), 10% of total ($6.00 min.)   _____

For shipping outside the Continental U.S. call 1-800-52-BOOKS for freight quote

Amount of check/money order enclosed   _____

Credit Card: Amex ____ Disc ____ MC ____ Visa ____

Account Number   _____

Exp. Date   _____

Signature   _____

Name _____

Address _____

City _____ State _____ Zip _____

Phone* _____ Date _____

*Required for all credit card orders.

Please visit our Web site, www.rizzoliusa.com, to download your copy of the illustrated calendar catalog.

Monday   **10**

Columbus Day (US)

Thanksgiving Day (Canada)

Tuesday   **11**

Full Moon

Wednesday   **12**

Thursday   **13**

Friday   **14**

Saturday   **15**   **Sunday**   **16**

OCTOBER

Monday   17

Tuesday   18

Wednesday   19

Thursday   20

Friday   21

Saturday   22   Sunday   23

OCTOBER

S	M	T	W	T	F	S
						1
2	3	4	5	6	7	8
9	10	11	12	13	14	15
16	17	18	19	20	21	22
23	24	25	26	27	28	29
30	31					

NOVEMBER

S	M	T	W	T	F	S
		1	2	3	4	5
6	7	8	9	10	11	12
13	14	15	16	17	18	19
20	21	22	23	24	25	26
27	28	29	30			

Beet Salad with Ricotta Salata and Olives

I'M CONVINCED that beets are best enjoyed in salads. The tang of a vinaigrette tames their earthy sweetness in a way that makes them easily likable. All varieties can be used in salads, and mixtures of red, golden, and striped Chioggas are dazzling. When mixing different colors, be sure to keep the red ones away from everything else until the end since they stain.

Serves 4 to 6

1 ¹/₂ LBS BEETS, STEAMED OR
ROASTED AND PEELED

1 SMALL GARLIC CLOVE

SALT

2 TSPS FRESH LEMON JUICE,
TO TASTE

2 TBSPS EXTRA-VIRGIN OLIVE
OIL

2 HANDFULS ARUGULA

4 OZS RICOTTA SALATA,
THINLY SLICED

8 KALAMATA OLIVES

Cut the beets into wedges or large dice, keeping different colors separate. Pound the garlic with ¹/₄ teaspoon salt in a mortar until smooth, then whisk in the lemon juice and olive oil. The dressing should be a little on the tart side. Toss the beets in enough dressing to coat lightly. Arrange them on a platter and garnish with arugula. Just before serving, tuck the cheese and olives among the greens. If any dressing remains, spoon it over the cheese.

The Spanish combination of anise with beets is just as right as the more familiar dill and orange. You can crush anise seeds in a mortar with garlic and salt, then whisk in sherry vinegar and olive oil (try a Spanish one if you haven't). Or you might introduce the anise flavor by lacing a vinaigrette with fresh leaves of anise hyssop or tarragon. Similarly, cilantro and lime are delicious with beets. The important element is not so much the herb, as the acid. Whether lemon, lime, or vinegar, the acid works to unite the sweet and earth flavors of the beets.

Butternut Squash Coins

BUTTERNUT SQUASH is the easiest and prettiest of the squashes to use because of its long, smooth neck. Serve these coins with sautéed onions, drizzled with Chermoula or salsa verde, or simply with plenty of freshly cracked pepper and a few drops of apple cider vinegar or balsamic vinegar.

Serves 4 to 6

1 LARGE BUTTERNUT SQUASH, ABOUT 3 LBS

3 TO 4 TBSPS OLIVE OIL OR SUNFLOWER SEED OIL

SALT AND FRESHLY GROUND BLACK PEPPER

Slice the neck from the squash where it joins the bulb. Peel it with a vegetable peeler or a knife, using long, even strokes. Slice the neck crosswise about $1/4$ inch thick. Reserve the bottom for another use. Preheat the oven to 200.

Heat 1 tablespoon of the oil in a wide skillet over medium-high heat. Add a single layer of squash and fry until golden and flecked with brown, about 10 minutes. Turn and fry the second side. Remove to paper towels to drain and keep warm in the oven. Repeat with the rest, adding oil as needed. Season with salt and pepper.

All-season grillers might try this: Cut the butternut squash into thick slices and steam them until barely tender. Brush them with olive oil to which you've added minced garlic, rosemary, and thyme, preferably fresh. Season each piece with salt and freshly ground pepper, then grill over ash-covered coals on both sides until marked and tender. Serve with a splash of your favorite vinegar.

Monday 24

Tuesday 25

Wednesday 26

Thursday 27

OCTOBER

S	M	T	W	T	F	S
						1
2	3	4	5	6	7	8
9	10	11	12	13	14	15
16	17	18	19	20	21	22
23	24	25	26	27	28	29
30	31					

NOVEMBER

S	M	T	W	T	F	S
		1	2	3	4	5
6	7	8	9	10	11	12
13	14	15	16	17	18	19
20	21	22	23	24	25	26
27	28	29	30			

Friday 28

Saturday 29

Sunday 30

OCTOBER / NOVEMBER

Monday **31**

Halloween

Tuesday **1**

Wednesday **2**

Thursday **3**

OCTOBER

S	M	T	W	T	F	S
						1
2	3	4	5	6	7	8
9	10	11	12	13	14	15
16	17	18	19	20	21	22
23	24	25	26	27	28	29
30	31					

Friday **4**

NOVEMBER

S	M	T	W	T	F	S
		1	2	3	4	5
6	7	8	9	10	11	12
13	14	15	16	17	18	19
20	21	22	23	24	25	26
27	28	29	30			

Saturday **5**

Sunday **6**

Daylight Saving Time Ends

Fingerling Potatoes with Slivered Garlic

THESE POTATOES end up moist and succulent, unless you continue baking them once they're tender—then they'll crisp on the bottom, and that's delicious, too.

Serves 4

3 TBSP BUTTER OR OLIVE OIL, PLUS MORE FOR THE DISH

1 LB FINGERLING OR OTHER POTATOES, SCRUBBED AND HALVED LENGTHWISE

6 GARLIC CLOVES, THINLY SLICED

SALT AND FRESHLY GROUND BLACK PEPPER

Preheat the oven to 400. Lightly butter a shallow baking dish. Layer the potatoes in the dish with the garlic and small pieces of butter or a drizzle of oil and season with salt and pepper.

Add a few tablespoons of water, cover with foil, and bake until tender, 40 to 50 minutes. Remove the foil and bake 15 minutes longer to brown the top.

Another approach to using the delicious fingerling potatoes you might find at your farmers' market is to bake them in salt. The salt leaves a distinct film of flavor but doesn't make them salty. Make a bed of coarse kosher salt or sea salt in a gratin dish or Dutch oven. Set scrubbed potatoes on the salt, cover with more salt, and bake in a 400-degree oven until the potatoes can be easily pierced with a knife about, 35 minutes. To serve the potatoes, scrape away the salt crust and gently dislodge the potatoes.

Monday   **7**

Tuesday   **8**

Election Day (US)

Wednesday   **9**

Thursday   **10**

Full Moon

Friday   **11**

Veterans Day (US)

Remembrance Day (Canada & UK)

Saturday   **12**

Sunday   **13**

NOVEMBER

S	M	T	W	T	F	S
		1	2	3	4	5
6	7	8	9	10	11	12
13	14	15	16	17	18	19
20	21	22	23	24	25	26
27	28	29	30			

DECEMBER

S	M	T	W	T	F	S
				1	2	3
4	5	6	7	8	9	10
11	12	13	14	15	16	17
18	19	20	21	22	23	24
25	26	27	28	29	30	31

NOVEMBER

Monday
14

Tuesday
15

Wednesday
16

Thursday
17

Friday
18

Saturday
19

Sunday
20

NOVEMBER

S	M	T	W	T	F	S
		1	2	3	4	5
6	7	8	9	10	11	12
13	14	15	16	17	18	19
20	21	22	23	24	25	26
27	28	29	30			

DECEMBER

S	M	T	W	T	F	S
				1	2	3
4	5	6	7	8	9	10
11	12	13	14	15	16	17
18	19	20	21	22	23	24
25	26	27	28	29	30	31

Seared Radicchio

A DELICIOUS ACCOMPANIMENT for soft polenta, cooked white beans, or an unusual ingredient for a risotto or hearty pasta.

Serves 4 to 6

2 SMALL, FIRM HEADS
  RADICCHIO, 3 TO 4 OZS
  EACH

OLIVE OIL AS NEEDED

SALT AND FRESHLY GROUND
  BLACK PEPPER

1 TBSP CHOPPED PARSLEY

PARMESAN, ASIAGO, OR DRY
  JACK CHEESE, THINLY
  SHAVED

Cut the radicchio into wedges about 2 inches thick at the widest point. Brush them generously with oil, season with salt and pepper, and set aside to marinate for an hour or more. Lightly film a cast-iron skillet with olive oil and set over medium-high heat. Once very hot, add the radicchio and sear until the leaves begin to brown on the bottom. Turn and cook the second side, about 5 minutes total. Transfer to a plate and gently press the wedges to open the leaves. Season with salt and pepper, sprinkle with parsley, and cover with shavings of cheese.

Escarole and Belgian endive can also be seared. While quite different in shape, size, and color, endive, radicchio, and escarole are all chicories—and as such they share a degree of bitterness that turns to sweetness when cooked. Use 2 heads of escarole and 2 to 4 endives, halved.

Golden Gratin of Carrots, Rutabagas, and Turnips

I CAN'T THINK OF any root vegetable that doesn't bake into a glorious gratin. Serve this one as a side dish or an entrée.

Serves 4

1 TBSP BUTTER, PLUS MORE
FOR THE DISH

BÉCHAMEL SAUCE FOR
GRATINS (SEE RIGHT)

12 OZS RUTABAGAS, PEELED
AND JULIENNED

SALT AND FRESHLY GROUND
BLACK PEPPER

1 SMALL ONION, FINELY DICED

12 OZS TURNIPS, PEELED AND
JULIENNED

8 OZS CARROTS, PEELED AND
JULIENNED

1 CUP FRESH BREAD CRUMBS

Preheat the oven to 375. Lightly butter a 2-quart gratin dish. Start the sauce, below. While it cooks, boil the rutabagas in salted water for 2 minutes, then drain. Cook the onion in the butter in a small skillet over medium heat, about 8 minutes; then combine with the rest of the vegetables. Season with salt and pepper and transfer to the gratin dish. Pour the sauce over the top, cover with the bread crumbs, and bake until bubbling and golden, about 45 minutes.

Béchamel Sauce for Gratins: Slowly heat 2 cups milk (or vegetable stock) in a saucepan with 2 slices onion, 8 sprigs parsley, 6 sprigs thyme, 2 bay leaves, and 1 crushed clove garlic. When it reaches a boil, remove from heat and set aside. In another saucepan, melt 4 tablespoons butter. Stir in 3 tablespoons flour and cook for 1 minute. Whisk in hot milk mixture. Cook until thickened, then transfer to a double boiler and cook, covered, for 25 minutes. Strain, discard the herbs, and season with salt, pepper, and a pinch of nutmeg. Stir in $1/2$ cup cream.

Monday

21

Tuesday

22

Wednesday

23

Thursday

24

Thanksgiving Day (US)

Friday

25

Saturday

26

Sunday

27

NOVEMBER

S	M	T	W	T	F	S
		1	2	3	4	5
6	7	8	9	10	11	12
13	14	15	16	17	18	19
20	21	22	23	24	25	26
27	28	29	30			

DECEMBER

S	M	T	W	T	F	S
				1	2	3
4	5	6	7	8	9	10
11	12	13	14	15	16	17
18	19	20	21	22	23	24
25	26	27	28	29	30	31

NOVEMBER / DECEMBER

Monday   28

Tuesday   29

Wednesday   30

Thursday   1

Friday   2

NOVEMBER						
S	M	T	W	T	F	S
		1	2	3	4	5
6	7	8	9	10	11	12
13	14	15	16	17	18	19
20	21	22	23	24	25	26
27	28	29	30			

DECEMBER						
S	M	T	W	T	F	S
				1	2	3
4	5	6	7	8	9	10
11	12	13	14	15	16	17
18	19	20	21	22	23	24
25	26	27	28	29	30	31

Saturday   3   Sunday   4

Roasted Mushrooms with Pine Nuts

ROASTING concentrates the earthy-woodsy flavor of mushrooms. Pine nuts are always good with mushrooms, especially when toasted.

Serves 4

1 LB CREMINI OR LARGE
WHITE MUSHROOMS,
SLICED ⅓ INCH THICK

SALT AND FRESHLY CRACKED
BLACK PEPPER

2 TO 3 TBSPS OLIVE OIL

3 TBSPS CHOPPED PARSLEY

2 GARLIC CLOVES

2 PINCHES RED PEPPER FLAKES

3 TBSPS TOASTED PINE NUTS

Preheat the oven to 400. Put the mushrooms in a wide, shallow baking dish, season with salt and pepper, and toss with the oil. Bake until sizzling, about 25 minutes. Meanwhile, chop the parsley and garlic together. When the mushrooms are done, toss them with the parsley mixture and pepper flakes. Scatter the pine nuts over the top and serve.

Instead of cutting mushrooms into even halves or quarters or slicing them in parallel lines, angle your knife to make the cuts irregular. Doing this reveals the interesting shapes and markings that even the most common mushrooms have, giving them more panache on the plate.

Monday

5

Tuesday

6

Wednesday

7

Thursday

8

DECEMBER 2011

S	M	T	W	T	F	S
				1	2	3
4	5	6	7	8	9	10
11	12	13	14	15	16	17
18	19	20	21	22	23	24
25	26	27	28	29	30	31

Friday

9

JANUARY 2012

S	M	T	W	T	F	S
1	2	3	4	5	6	7
8	9	10	11	12	13	14
15	16	17	18	19	20	21
22	23	24	25	26	27	28
29	30	31				

Saturday

10

Human Rights Day

Full Moon

Sunday

11

DECEMBER

Monday   12

Tuesday   13

Wednesday   14

Thursday   15

DECEMBER 2011

S	M	T	W	T	F	S
				1	2	3
4	5	6	7	8	9	10
11	12	13	14	15	16	17
18	19	20	21	22	23	24
25	26	27	28	29	30	31

Friday   16

JANUARY 2012

S	M	T	W	T	F	S
1	2	3	4	5	6	7
8	9	10	11	12	13	14
15	16	17	18	19	20	21
22	23	24	25	26	27	28
29	30	31				

Saturday   17   Sunday   18

Chard Rolls with Winter Vegetables

SELECT nice, large leaves for stuffing. The chard stems along with root vegetables fill these plump bundles.

Serves 4

2 TBSPS OLIVE OIL

8 LARGE CHARD LEAVES, STEMS REMOVED AND FINELY DICED

1 ONION, FINELY DICED

3 CARROTS, FINELY DICED

8 OZS POTATOES, FINELY DICED

6 TO 8 CUPS ADDITIONAL VEGETABLES, FINELY DICED, SUCH AS CELERY ROOT, PARSLEY ROOT, AND PARSNIPS

1 GARLIC CLOVE, MINCED

2 TSPS CHOPPED TARRAGON OR $^1/_2$ TSP DRIED

SALT AND FRESHLY GROUND BLACK PEPPER

2 TBSPS FRESH LEMON JUICE

1 CUP WATER OR VEGETABLE STOCK

1 TO 2 TBSPS BUTTER

Heat the oil in a large skillet. Add the chard stems, onion, other root vegetables, garlic, and tarragon. Season with $^1/_2$ teaspoon salt and pepper to taste. Cover and cook over medium heat until tender, 20 to 25 minutes. Add the lemon juice and taste for salt.

Plunge the chard leaves into boiling water for 4 minutes, then set them on a towel to drain. Cut away the thick part at the base of each leaf. Place the leaves, smooth side down, on a work surface. Place 2 heaping tablespoons of the filling just above the notch of each leaf, then fold the sides over and roll up the leaves. Keep the remaining filling in the skillet and set the rolls right on top of it. Add the water to the pan, dot the leaves with the butter, and cover. Simmer for 10 minutes. Serve the rolls with the extra vegetables and their juices.

Brussels Sprouts and Walnuts with Fennel and Red Pearl Onions

THIS GORGEOUS DISH was inspired by Patricia Wells. It's a bit of an effort, best perhaps for a holiday meal.

Serves 8 or more

1 CUP WALNUT HALVES

1 PINT RED PEARL ONIONS OR SHALLOTS

2 TBSPS BUTTER

1 TBSP SUGAR

SALT AND FRESHLY GROUND BLACK PEPPER

1 FENNEL BULB, JULIENNED

1 CUP VEGETABLE STOCK OR WATER

3 TBSPS CHOPPED PARSLEY AND CELERY LEAVES, MIXED

1 LB BRUSSELS SPROUTS, LEFT WHOLE IF SMALL, HALVED OR QUARTERED IF LARGE

2 TBSPS WALNUT OIL

2 TBSPS CHOPPED FENNEL GREENS AND PARSLEY, MIXED

Drop the walnuts into a pan of boiling water for 1 minute, then remove. Rub off what you can of their skins with a towel, then dry in a 350-degree oven for 7 to 8 minutes. Scald the onions in the same water for 1 minute, then drain. Slip off the outer skins without cutting off the root end. If using shallots, peel and separate following their natural divisions.

Melt half the butter in a skillet over medium heat. Add the onions, sprinkle with the sugar, and season with salt and pepper. Cover and cook over low heat, shaking the pan occasionally, until the onions are lightly browned and nearly tender, about 12 minutes. Add the fennel and cook, covered, until tender, another 8 to 10 minutes.

Melt the remaining butter in a second skillet. Add the walnuts and cook over low heat, shaking the pan occasionally, until golden, 12 to 15 minutes. Add the stock and parsley-celery leaves mixture. Simmer, covered, until liquid reduces to a few tablespoons. Taste for seasoning and combine with onion and fennel mixture.

Boil the Brussels sprouts in salted water until tender, 6 to 8 minutes, then add them to the mixture. Add the walnut oil and fennel-parsley mixture, gently stir everything together, and serve.

This is an elaborate preparation for a special meal, but you can cook everything except the Brussels sprouts the day before. Reheat the vegetables, blanch the sprouts, and combine them just before serving.

DECEMBER

Monday 19

Tuesday 20

Hanukkah (Begins at Sundown)

Wednesday 21

Thursday 22

First Day of Winter

Friday 23

DECEMBER 2011

S	M	T	W	T	F	S
				1	2	3
4	5	6	7	8	9	10
11	12	13	14	15	16	17
18	19	20	21	22	23	24
25	26	27	28	29	30	31

JANUARY 2012

S	M	T	W	T	F	S
1	2	3	4	5	6	7
8	9	10	11	12	13	14
15	16	17	18	19	20	21
22	23	24	25	26	27	28
29	30	31				

Saturday 24

Sunday 25

Christmas

DECEMBER 2011 / JANUARY 2012

Monday **26**

Kwanzaa Begins

Boxing Day (Canada & UK)

Tuesday **27**

Bank Holiday (UK)

Wednesday **28**

Thursday **29**

Friday **30**

Saturday **31**

Sunday **1**

New Year's Day

Spaghettini with Cauliflower, Butter, and Pepper

THE SIMPLICITY of this dish is deceiving. It's full of warm, lively flavors.

Serves 4 to 6

SALT AND FRESHLY GROUND
  BLACK PEPPER

1 CAULIFLOWER, CUT INTO
  TINY FLORETS, STEMS
  PEELED AND CHOPPED

3 TO 4 TBSPS BUTTER

$^1/_2$ CUP FINELY CHOPPED
  PARSLEY

1 TSP COARSE MUSTARD

$^1/_4$ TSP RED PEPPER FLAKES

1 LB SPAGHETTINI,
  ORECCHIETTE, OR SMALL
  CONCHIGLIE

$^1/_2$ CUP FRESHLY GRATED
  PARMESAN, PECORINO
  ROMANO, OR A MIXTURE

$^1/_2$ CUP FRESH BREAD CRUMBS,
  TOASTED UNTIL CRISP AND
  GOLDEN

Bring a large pot of water to a rolling boil. Salt to taste, add the cauliflower, and cook for 3 minutes. Scoop the cauliflower into a large pasta bowl and add the butter, parsley, mustard, and pepper flakes. Add the pasta to the water and set the bowl over the pot to keep it warm, leaving a crack so the water doesn't boil over. Drain the pasta and add it to the cauliflower. Grind a generous amount of pepper over all, then toss with the cheese and bread crumbs.

The complex, warm flavors of curry powders are especially good with cauliflower. Skip the pasta in this dish and steam or blanch the cauliflower. Warm several tablespoons butter in a skillet with a teaspoon or more curry powder, fresh lime juice, snipped chives, and chopped cilantro leaves. Toss with the cauliflower and garnish with toasted cashews.

Notes

2011

JANUARY
S	M	T	W	T	F	S
						1
2	3	4	5	6	7	8
9	10	11	12	13	14	15
16	17	18	19	20	21	22
23	24	25	26	27	28	29
30	31					

FEBRUARY
S	M	T	W	T	F	S
		1	2	3	4	5
6	7	8	9	10	11	12
13	14	15	16	17	18	19
20	21	22	23	24	25	26
27	28					

MARCH
S	M	T	W	T	F	S
		1	2	3	4	5
6	7	8	9	10	11	12
13	14	15	16	17	18	19
20	21	22	23	24	25	26
27	28	29	30	31		

APRIL
S	M	T	W	T	F	S
					1	2
3	4	5	6	7	8	9
10	11	12	13	14	15	16
17	18	19	20	21	22	23
24	25	26	27	28	29	30

MAY
S	M	T	W	T	F	S
1	2	3	4	5	6	7
8	9	10	11	12	13	14
15	16	17	18	19	20	21
22	23	24	25	26	27	28
29	30	31				

JUNE
S	M	T	W	T	F	S
			1	2	3	4
5	6	7	8	9	10	11
12	13	14	15	16	17	18
19	20	21	22	23	24	25
26	27	28	29	30		

JULY
S	M	T	W	T	F	S
					1	2
3	4	5	6	7	8	9
10	11	12	13	14	15	16
17	18	19	20	21	22	23
24	25	26	27	28	29	30
31						

AUGUST
S	M	T	W	T	F	S
	1	2	3	4	5	6
7	8	9	10	11	12	13
14	15	16	17	18	19	20
21	22	23	24	25	26	27
28	29	30	31			

SEPTEMBER
S	M	T	W	T	F	S
				1	2	3
4	5	6	7	8	9	10
11	12	13	14	15	16	17
18	19	20	21	22	23	24
25	26	27	28	29	30	

OCTOBER
S	M	T	W	T	F	S
						1
2	3	4	5	6	7	8
9	10	11	12	13	14	15
16	17	18	19	20	21	22
23	24	25	26	27	28	29
30	31					

NOVEMBER
S	M	T	W	T	F	S
		1	2	3	4	5
6	7	8	9	10	11	12
13	14	15	16	17	18	19
20	21	22	23	24	25	26
27	28	29	30			

DECEMBER
S	M	T	W	T	F	S
				1	2	3
4	5	6	7	8	9	10
11	12	13	14	15	16	17
18	19	20	21	22	23	24
25	26	27	28	29	30	31

2012

JANUARY
S	M	T	W	T	F	S
1	2	3	4	5	6	7
8	9	10	11	12	13	14
15	16	17	18	19	20	21
22	23	24	25	26	27	28
29	30	31				

FEBRUARY
S	M	T	W	T	F	S
			1	2	3	4
5	6	7	8	9	10	11
12	13	14	15	16	17	18
19	20	21	22	23	24	25
26	27	28	29			

MARCH
S	M	T	W	T	F	S
				1	2	3
4	5	6	7	8	9	10
11	12	13	14	15	16	17
18	19	20	21	22	23	24
25	26	27	28	29	30	31

APRIL
S	M	T	W	T	F	S
1	2	3	4	5	6	7
8	9	10	11	12	13	14
15	16	17	18	19	20	21
22	23	24	25	26	27	28
29	30					

MAY
S	M	T	W	T	F	S
		1	2	3	4	5
6	7	8	9	10	11	12
13	14	15	16	17	18	19
20	21	22	23	24	25	26
27	28	29	30	31		

JUNE
S	M	T	W	T	F	S
					1	2
3	4	5	6	7	8	9
10	11	12	13	14	15	16
17	18	19	20	21	22	23
24	25	26	27	28	29	30

JULY
S	M	T	W	T	F	S
1	2	3	4	5	6	7
8	9	10	11	12	13	14
15	16	17	18	19	20	21
22	23	24	25	26	27	28
29	30	31				

AUGUST
S	M	T	W	T	F	S
			1	2	3	4
5	6	7	8	9	10	11
12	13	14	15	16	17	18
19	20	21	22	23	24	25
26	27	28	29	30	31	

SEPTEMBER
S	M	T	W	T	F	S
						1
2	3	4	5	6	7	8
9	10	11	12	13	14	15
16	17	18	19	20	21	22
23	24	25	26	27	28	29
30						

OCTOBER
S	M	T	W	T	F	S
	1	2	3	4	5	6
7	8	9	10	11	12	13
14	15	16	17	18	19	20
21	22	23	24	25	26	27
28	29	30	31			

NOVEMBER
S	M	T	W	T	F	S
				1	2	3
4	5	6	7	8	9	10
11	12	13	14	15	16	17
18	19	20	21	22	23	24
25	26	27	28	29	30	

DECEMBER
S	M	T	W	T	F	S
						1
2	3	4	5	6	7	8
9	10	11	12	13	14	15
16	17	18	19	20	21	22
23	24	25	26	27	28	29
30	31					